Bones

'Bones'
An original concept by Jill Atkins
© Jill Atkins 2022

Illustrated by Gareth Robinson

Published by MAVERICK ARTS PUBLISHING LTD
Studio 11, City Business Centre, 6 Brighton Road,
Horsham, West Sussex, RH13 5BB
© Maverick Arts Publishing Limited August 2022
+44 (0)1403 256941

A CIP catalogue record for this book is available at the British Library.

ISBN 978-1-84886-898-4

www.maverickbooks.co.uk

This book is rated as: Orange Band (Guided Reading)
It follows the requirements for Phase 5 phonics.
Most words are decodable, and any non-decodable words are familiar,
supported by the context and/or represented in the artwork.

Bones

By Jill Atkins

Illustrated by
Gareth Robinson

One Monday morning, a skeleton stepped out of his deep, dark cave.

He was called Bones. He grinned to himself with his perfect white teeth.

Bones set off along the road on long,

thin legs.

Clink! Clink!

A little dog, called Punk, followed him.

Punk barked.

It made Bones jump.

One of his teeth fell

out. Plink!

It clattered to the

ground.

"Oh dear," said Bones. "I've lost a tooth."

Punk grabbed the tooth in her mouth.

She ran off, dug a little hole and dropped

the tooth in.

On Tuesday, Bones went to the park.

Punk followed.

Bones threw sticks for Punk to fetch.

They had so much fun!

Suddenly, one of his fingers fell off.

Plunk!

"Oh no!" he cried. "I've lost a finger."

Punk gripped the finger in her mouth.

She dashed away, dug another hole

and popped the finger in.

On Wednesday, Bones went up a steep hill.
Punk fetched lots of sticks, which Bones
threw for her.

Then, Bones slipped. One of his ribs fell off.

Clonk!

"Oh bother!" he exclaimed. "I've lost a rib.

Never mind. I've got plenty more."

Punk clenched the rib in her mouth.

She scampered off, dug a big hole and hid

the rib.

On Thursday, Bones went to the shops.

Punk was close behind.

Bones had just reached up for a hat when his hand fell off. Clank!

"Oh gosh!"

he muttered.

"I've lost a hand."

Punk picked up the hand with her mouth.

She ran outside, dug a hole and hid the hand.

On Friday, Bones skipped to the farm.

Punk followed.

Bones played with Punk, but then

he trod in thick mud.

When he lifted his leg, his foot was stuck in the mud.

"Oh my goodness!" he sighed. "I've lost a foot."

Punk pulled out the foot. She went behind the barn and hid it in a hole in the ground.

Bones looked for his missing bones, but he couldn't find them.
Then, he hopped home.

On Saturday, Bones stayed at home.

"I've lost my tooth, my finger, my hand,

my rib and my foot," he said.

He looked sad.

Punk felt sad too.

Now Bones could not go for a walk and throw sticks for her to fetch.

On Sunday, Punk ran from hole to hole.

She collected all the bones she had hidden.

Then, she ran to Bones in his cave.

"My bones!" Bones gasped.

Punk stuck the missing bones back in place.

"Thank you, Punk!" Bones grinned.

Then, Bones stood up and stamped his feet.

"I feel so much better," he cheered.

"Let's go for a walk, Punk," said Bones.

"You can help me keep my bones safe now!"

"Woof!" Punk barked happily.

Quiz

1. What did Bones do on Tuesday?
a) He went to the park
b) He went to the beach
c) He stayed at home

2. On Wednesday, Bones went up a
_____ hill.
a) high
b) long
c) steep

3. How did Bones lose his foot?
a) It rolled down a hill
b) It got stuck in mud
c) It was taken by a bird

4. How many bones did Bones lose?

a) Three

b) Five

c) Ten

5. Where were the bones hidden?

a) In the cave

b) In holes

c) In mud

Turn over for answers

Book Bands for Guided Reading

The Institute of Education book banding system is a scale of colours that reflects the various levels of reading difficulty. The bands are assigned by taking into account the content, the language style, the layout and phonics. Word, phrase and sentence level work is also taken into consideration.

Maverick Early Readers are a bright, attractive range of books covering the pink to white bands. All of these books have been book banded for guided reading to the industry standard and edited by a leading educational consultant.

To view the whole Maverick Readers scheme, visit our website at www.maverickearlyreaders.com

Or scan the QR code above to view our scheme instantly!

Quiz Answers: 1a, 2c, 3b, 4b, 5b